The Garden

written by Karen Hoenecke
illustrated by Jenny Campbell

KAEDEN ♥ BOOKS™

Grandma and Grandpa were going to plant a garden.

Grandma wanted to plant flowers. Grandpa wanted to plant vegetables.

They decided to share the garden.

Grandpa planted tomato seeds in part of the garden.

He planted carrot seeds in another part of the garden.

He also planted bean seeds and corn seeds.

Grandma planted flower seeds in her part of the garden.

The seeds got water.
The seeds got light.
The garden started to grow.

Grandpa thought about how good the vegetables would taste.

Grandma thought about beautiful flowers.

The sprouts got water.
The sprouts got light.
The garden grew and grew.

Grandpa thought about how good the vegetables would taste.

Grandma thought of beautiful flowers.

The plants got water.
The plants got light.
The garden grew and grew
and grew.

Grandpa thought about how good the vegetables would taste.

Grandma thought of beautiful flowers.

Then one day, the bugs tasted the tomatoes.

The rabbits tasted the carrots.

The birds tasted the beans.

The deer tasted the corn.

Grandpa thought about the bugs, the rabbits, the birds and the deer tasting his vegetables.

Grandma comforted Grandpa. Then she went . . .

. . . to pick her beautiful flowers!